Table of Contents

INTRODUCTION

The air fryer is a kitchen appliance that promises to slash the fat in many dishes that you would typically pan fry or deep fry. In other words, you can achieve an impressive batch of "fried" chicken and French fries without cups of cooking oil when you cook them in an air fryer.

An air fryer is essentially a miniature convection oven that evenly circulates hot air around your food. Air fryers contain a fan that rapidly moves the heated air around, helping your food to crisp up without much additional oil. It also has the ability to reach very high temperatures (with some models getting up to 430F°) enhancing its ability to quickly cook foods. The device is ideal for anyone keeping a close eye on their fat consumption, as you only need a thin coat of oil on the food or on the cookware surface to prevent sticking and achieve a golden, crispy crunch. Not only does it fry, but the air fryer can also mimic other cooking functions such as baking, grilling and roasting.

Keep in mind that an air fryer is ideal for making foods in small quantities simply because the appliance does not have the physical capacity to hold a lot of food at one time. Most models can hold a from 3.5 quarts to 5.5 quarts in their fry baskets. The fry basket is the main accessory that comes with an air fryer, but some models can include other elements such as a baking pan or roasting rack. Being that the air fryer is similar to a convection oven (but way smaller), it can save you time (and electricity) over heating up your standard oven.

Do Air Fryers Need Oil?

Air fryers work by using high heat (around 320-400 degrees Fahrenheit and 160 - 205 degrees centigrade) to cook food. Because of this, you can expect fast cooking times but also a crisp finish to your dishes. The high heat and convection technology mean you won't need a load of oil to cook your food properly either. You can place frozen food or raw vegetables and meat into the basket of the air fryer, and then close the lid to allow the machine to retain its heat and prevent the room you're cooking in from becoming hot, rather than your actual food.

These handy appliances also remove the need to preheat food as the high temperatures will cut down cooking time, and without oil, these machines don't create the odors you'd typically associate with deep fryers. Since you won't be submerging your food into a vat of oil, you also won't need to worry about splashing hot oil onto yourself when you take your food out. Once your air fryer has finished cooking, you can simply remove the cooking basket and tip your food out, ready to serve.

If you're wondering what your food will look like if you use an air fryer, you can still expect crisp, tasty results that you'd get from deep frying, but without the greasiness. Compared to traditional cooking in an oven, air frying will create a more crispy result.

Is Air-Fried Food Healthy?

You could argue that air-fried food is healthier than deep-fried food because it uses less oil. Frozen french fries prepared in the air fryer contain between 4 and 6 grams of fat versus their deep-fried counterparts, which have a whopping 17 grams per serving.

Advantages of Air Fryer

- Air Fryer are Easier to Clean Than Deep Fryers

  An air fryer is easy to clean up since it has dishwasher-safe parts. The parts are the basket, the tray and the pan which are washed similar to how you do other dishes: with soap and hot water. Apart from this, you may need to use a comgortable bristle brush to keep your air fryer sparkling all the time.

- Air fryers remove fat from food

Air fryers use very little oil to cook. Even air fryers can cook food without oil. Foods cooked in other cooking methods contain high fat. As a result, food cooked in all these ways is not healthy. Many manufacturers claim that their air fryer removes up to 95% fat from fried foods.

Moreover, the air fryer cooks using very little oil compared to the traditional frying method. While many recipes require 3 cups of oil to cook in the traditional frying method, only 1 teaspoon of oil is required to cook the same recipe in an air fryer. However, the taste of food does not change much.

Air fryers use a special type of technology to remove excess fat from food that traps fat from food and stores it under the air fryer basket. Various experiments have shown that air fryers can cook delicious fried foods like the traditional frying method with very little oil. Which makes the food delicious and healthy at the same time.

- To lose weight

Traditional fried foods not only contain extra fat but also extra calories. Excess calories will increase your weight. So if you want to lose weight, you should avoid fried foods. However, food cooked through an air fryer is extra calorie-free. Because air fryers use very little oil to cook fried food. With an air fryer, you can lose weight without avoiding fried foods.

- An air fryer uses little to no oil to cooks food

  Cooking in traditional deep fryers often takes up to a gallon of oil. But it takes just one tablespoon of oil to cook any recipe in an air fryer. Moreover, many recipes can be cooked without oil.

- Take little space

  Air fryers are usually small in size. As a result, they do not require much space in the kitchen. These are much smaller than other kitchen appliances. Air fryers are usually slightly larger than a coffee maker and smaller than a toaster oven. However, air fryers of different sizes are available in the market. You can buy small-size air fryers for small families and big-size air fryers for big families. All types of air fryers, small or large, do not require much space to be placed on the countertop.

RECIPES

Air Fryer Banana Bread

Prep Time: 15 minutes

Total Time: 45 minutes

Servings: 8

Ingredients:

- 3/4 cup (3 oz.) white-whole wheat flour
- 1 teaspoon cinnamon
- 1/2 teaspoon Kosher salt
- 1/4 teaspoon Baking soda
- 2 medium (12 oz. total) ripe bananas, mashed (about 3/4 cup)
- 2 large eggs, lightly beaten
- 1/2 cup granulated sugar

- 1/3 cup plain nonfat yogurt
- 2 tablespoons vegetable oil
- 1 teaspoon Vanilla extract
- 2 tablespoons (3/4 oz.) toasted walnuts, roughly chopped
- Cooking spray

Directions:

1. Line the bottom of a 6-inch round cake pan with parchment paper; lightly coat pan with cooking spray. Whisk together flour, cinnamon, salt and baking soda in a medium bowl; set aside.
2. In separate medium bowl, whisk together mashed bananas, eggs, sugar, yogurt, oil and vanilla. Gently stir wet ingredients into flour mixture until well combined. Pour

batter into prepared pan and sprinkle with walnuts.

3. Heat a 5.3-qt air fryer to 310°F and then place pan in air fryer and cook until browned and a wooden pick inserted in the middle comes out clean, 30 to 35 minutes, turning pan halfway through cook time. Transfer bread to a wire rack to cool in pan for 15 minutes before turning out and slicing.

Nutrition Facts:

Calories 180 | Fat 6g | Protein 4g | Carbohydrate 29g | Fiber 2g | Sugars 17g

Air Fryer Churros With Chocolate Sauce

Total Time: 1 hour 25 minutes

Servings: 12

Ingredients:

- 1/2 cup water
- 1/4 teaspoon kosher salt
- 1/4 cup , plus 2 Tbsp. unsalted butter, divided
- 1/2 cup (about 2 1/8 oz.) all-purpose flour
- 2 large eggs
- 1/3 cup granulated sugar
- 2 teaspoons ground cinnamon
- 4 ounces bittersweet baking chocolate, finely chopped
- 3 tablespoons heavy cream

- 2 tablespoons vanilla kefir

Directions:

1. Bring water, salt, and 1/4 cup of the butter to a boil in a small saucepan over medium-high. Reduce heat to medium-low; add flour, and stir vigorously with a wooden spoon until dough is smooth, about 30 seconds. Continue cooking, stirring constantly, until dough begins to pull away from sides of pan and a film forms on bottom of pan, 2 to 3 minutes. Transfer dough to a medium bowl. Stir constantly until slightly cooled, about 1 minute. Add eggs, 1 at a time, stirring constantly until completely smooth after each addition. Transfer mixture to a piping bag fitted with a medium star tip. Chill 30 minutes.

2. Pipe 6 (3-inch long) pieces in single layer in air fryer basket. Cook at 380°F until golden, about 10 minutes. Repeat with remaining dough.
3. Stir together sugar and cinnamon in a medium bowl. Brush cooked churros with remaining 2 tablespoons melted butter, and roll in sugar mixture to coat.
4. Place chocolate and cream in a small microwavable bowl. Microwave on HIGH until melted and smooth, about 30 seconds, stirring after 15 seconds. Stir in kefir. Serve churros with chocolate sauce.

Nutrition Facts:

Calories 173 | Fat 11g | Protein 3g | Carbohydrate 12g | Fiber 1g | Sugars 7g

Air Fryer Southern Style Catfish With Green Beans

Total Time: 25 minutes

Servings: 2

Ingredients:

- 12 ounces fresh green beans, trimmed
- Cooking spray
- 1 teaspoon light brown sugar
- 1/2 teaspoon crushed red pepper (optional)
- 3/8 teaspoon kosher salt, divided
- 2 Unit (6-oz.) catfish fillets
- 1/4 cup all-purpose flour
- 1 large egg, lightly beaten
- 1/3 cup panko (Japanese-style breadcrumbs)

- 1/4 teaspoon black pepper
- 2 tablespoons mayonnaise
- 1 1/2 teaspoons finely chopped fresh dill
- 3/4 teaspoon dill pickle relish
- 1/2 teaspoon apple cider vinegar
- 1/8 teaspoon granulated sugar
- Lemon wedges

Directions:

1. Place green beans in a medium bowl, and spray liberally with cooking spray. Sprinkle with brown sugar, crushed red pepper (if using), and 1/8 teaspoon of the salt. Place in air fryer basket, and cook at 400ºF until well browned and tender, about 12 minutes. Transfer to a bowl; cover with aluminum foil to keep warm.

2. Meanwhile, toss catfish in flour to coat, shaking excess from fish. Dip pieces, 1 at a time, in egg to coat, then sprinkle with panko, pressing to coat evenly on all sides. Place

3. fish in air fryer basket; spray with cooking spray. Cook at 400ºF until browned and cooked through, about 8 minutes. Sprinkle tops evenly with pepper and remaining 1/4 teaspoon salt.

4. While fish is cooking, whisk together mayonnaise, dill, relish, vinegar, and sugar in a small bowl. Serve fish and green beans with tartar sauce and lemon wedges.

Nutrition Facts:

Calories 416 | Fat 18g | Protein 33g | Carbohydrate 31g | Fiber 7g | Sugars 8g

Air Fryer Strawberry Pop Tarts

Total Time: 2 hours

Servings: 6

Ingredients:

- 8 ounces quartered strawberries (about 1 3/4 cups)
- 1/4 cup granulated sugar
- 1/2 (14.1-oz.) pkg. refrigerated piecrusts
- Cooking spray
- 1/2 cup (about 2 oz.) powdered sugar
- 1 1/2 teaspoons fresh lemon juice (from 1 lemon)
- 1/2 ounce rainbow candy sprinkles (about 1 Tbsp.)

Directions:

1. Stir together strawberries and granulated sugar in medium microwavable bowl. Let stand 15 minutes, stirring occasionally. Microwave on HIGH until shiny and reduced, about 10 minutes, stirring halfway through cooking. Cool completely, about 30 minutes.
2. Roll pie crust into a 12-inch circle on a lightly floured surface. Cut dough into 12 (2 1/2- x 3-inch) rectangles, rerolling scraps, if needed. Spoon about 2 teaspoons strawberry mixture into center of 6 of the dough rectangles, leaving a 1/2-inch border. Brushes edges of filled dough rectangles with water; top with remaining dough rectangles, pressing edges with a

fork to seal. Coat tarts well with cooking spray.

3. Place 3 tarts in single layer in air fryer basket, and cook at 350°F until golden brown, about 10 minutes. Repeat with remaining tarts. Place on a wire rack to cool completely, about 30 minutes.
4. Whisk together powdered sugar and lemon juice in a small bowl until smooth. Spoon glaze over cooled tarts, and sprinkle evenly with candy sprinkles.

Nutrition Facts:

Calories 229 l Fat 9g | Protein 2g | Carbohydrate 39g | Fiber 1g | Sugars 22g

Air-Fried Peach Hand Pies

Total Time: 1 hour

Servings: 8

Ingredients:

- 2 (5-oz.) fresh peaches, peeled and chopped
- 1 tablespoon fresh lemon juice (from 1 lemon)
- 3 tablespoons granulated sugar
- 1 teaspoon vanilla extract
- 1/4 teaspoon table salt
- 1 teaspoon cornstarch
- 1 (14.1-oz.) pkg. refrigerated piecrusts
- Cooking spray

Directions:

1. Stir together peaches, lemon juice, sugar, vanilla, and salt a in medium bowl. Let stand 15 minutes, stirring occasionally. Drain peaches, reserving 1 tablespoon liquid. Whisk cornstarch into reserved liquid; stir into drained peaches.
2. Cut piecrusts into 8 (4-inch) circles. Place about 1 tablespoon filling in center of each circle. Brush edges of dough with water; fold dough over filling to form half-moons. Crimp edges with a fork to seal; cut 3 small slits in top of pies. Coat pies well with cooking spray.
3. Place 3 pies in single layer in air fryer basket, and cook at 350°F until golden brown, 12 to 14 minutes. Repeat with remaining pies.

Nutrition Facts:

Calories 314 | Fat 16g | Protein 3g | Carbohydrate 43g | Fiber 1g | Sugars 10g

Air Fryer Fried Green Tomatoes

Prep Time: 5 minutes

Cook Time: 8 minutes

Total Time: 13 minutes

Servings: 4

Ingredients:

- 2 green tomatoes, (3 if they are smaller)
- salt and pepper
- 1/2 cup all-purpose flour
- 2 large eggs
- 1/2 cup buttermilk
- 1 cup Panko crumbs
- 1 cup yellow cornmeal
- n=mister filled with olive oil or vegetable oil

Directions:

1. Cut tomatoes into 1/4-inch slices. Pat dry with paper towels and season well with salt and pepper.
2. Place flour in a shallow dish or pie plate, or for easy clean-up use a paper plate.
3. Whisk together eggs and buttermilk in a shallow dish or bowl.
4. Combine Panko crumbs and cornmeal in a shallow dish or pie plate, or for easy clean-up use a paper plate.
5. Preheat air fryer to 400 degrees.
6. Coat the tomato slices in the flour, dip in egg mixture, and then press panko crumb mixture into both sides. Sprinkle a little more salt on them.

7. Mist air fryer basket with oil and place 4 tomato slices in basket. Mist the tops with oil. Air-fry for 5 minutes.
8. Flip tomatoes over, mist with oil and air-fry 3 more minutes.
9. Serve with Comeback sauce if desired.

Air Fried Potatoes

Prep Time: 5 minutes

Cook Time: 20 minutes

Soaking Time: 45 minutes

Total Time: 1 hour 10 minutes

Servings: 2

Ingredients:

- 2 medium Russet Potatoes
- 1/2 tsp salt
- 1 Tbsp olive oil
- 1/4 tsp garlic powder
- chopped parsley for garnish

Directions:

1. Clean and scrub potatoes under running water. Dice potatoes into 1/2 inch cubes.
2. Place potatoes in bowl and cover with ice cold water. Allow to soak for 45 minutes.
3. Remove potatoes from water and dry with paper towels. Add potatoes in dry bowl and add olive oil, salt, garlic powder. Stir potatoes ensuring that all pieces are covered in oil.
4. Place in air fryer basket. Cook at 400 degrees Farenheit 20-23 minutes, shaking the basket halfway through. Potatoes are done when they are golden brown on the outside and soft on the inside.
5. Top with parsley if desired.

Air Fryer Zucchini Fritters

Prep Time: 12 minutes

Cook Time: 12 minutes

Total Time: 24 minutes

Servings: 4

Ingredients:

- 2 medium/large zucchini
- 1 Tbsp kosher salt
- 1 large egg
- 3 Tbsp All purpose flour
- 1 tsp garlic powder
- ¼ tsp onion powder
- ¼ tsp paprika
- ¼ tsp black pepper

- Oil for spraying

Herb Dip:

- 1/4 cup Greek Yogurt or Sour Cream
- 2 Tbsp fresh herbs
- 2 tsp minced garlic
- 1 tsp Lemon juice
- salt to taste

Directions:

1. Wash, dry, and cut off the ends of zucchini. Use large scale side of a box grater to grate the zucchini.
2. Add 1 Tbsp of salt and stir it into the grated zucchini. Allow it to rest for 10 minutes.

3. Meanwhile, prepare dip by combine greek yogurt or sour cream, lemon juice, salt, and chopped herbs to a bowl. Set aside.
4. After 10 minutes, use a good quality paper towel to squeeze excess water our of zucchini until it is dry. Place in a clean and dry bowl.
5. Add egg, all-purpose flour, garlic powder, onion powder, paprika, and black pepper to zucchini and stir.
6. Place a parchment liner in the Air Fryer basket or grease it with oil to avoid sticking. Place zucchini mixture on the paper liner by the spoonful, about 1 inch apart. Lightly spray with oil.

7. Close Air Fryer and cook on 360 degrees Fahrenheit for 12 minutes, flipping and spraying halfway through.

Nutrition Facts:

Calories: 57kcal | Carbohydrates: 8g | Protein: 3g | Fat: 1g | Saturated Fat: 1g | Cholesterol: 41mg | Sodium: 1768mg | Potassium: 280mg | Fiber: 1g | Sugar: 3g | Vitamin A: 325IU | Vitamin C: 17.6mg | Calcium: 22mg | Iron: 0.8mg

Easy Peel Air Fryer Hard Boiled Eggs

Prep Time: 1 minutes

Cook Time: 15 minutes

Ice Bath: 5 minutes

Total Time: 21 minutes

Ingredients:

- 1-6 large eggs

Directions:

1. Preheat Air Fryer to 270 degrees Fahrenheit.
2. Place eggs in Air Fryer basket. Close and cook on 270 degrees Fahrenheit for 15 minutes. Once timer is done, remove from Air Fryer basket and place in bowl filled with ice water for 5 minutes.

3. Remove, peel, and Enjoy

Nutrition Facts:

Calories: 62kcal | Protein: 5g | Fat: 4g | Saturated Fat: 1g | Cholesterol: 163mg | Sodium: 62mg | Potassium: 60mg | Vitamin A: 240IU | Calcium: 25mg | Iron: 0.8mg

Air Fryer Egg Frittata

Prep Time: 10 minutes

Cook Time: 15 minutes

Total Time: 25 minutes

Servings: 2

Ingredients:

- 4 eggs
- ½ cup milk
- 2 green onions chopped
- ¼ cup baby bella mushrooms chopped
- ¼ cup spinach chopped
- ¼ cup red bell pepper chopped
- ¼ cup cheddar cheese
- ½ tsp salt

- ½ tsp black pepper
- Dash of hot sauce

Directions:

1. Grease 6x3 inch round or square pan with butter. Set aside.
2. Whisk eggs and milk in a large bowl until blended. Stir in green onions, mushrooms, spinach, red bell pepper, cheddar cheese, salt, black pepper, and hot sauce.
3. Pour egg mixture into greased pan.
4. Place in air fryer and cook on 360 degrees Fahrenheit for 15-18 minutes, or until a toothpick comes out clean.

Notes:

- Cook times will depend on Air Fryer model.
- You can grease your pan with oil or butter.

Nutrition Facts:

Calories: 233kcal | Carbohydrates: 6g | Protein: 17g | Fat: 15g | Saturated Fat: 6g | Cholesterol: 348mg | Sodium: 826mg | Potassium: 335mg | Sugar: 4g | Vitamin A: 1770IU | Vitamin C: 27.1mg | Calcium: 229mg | Iron: 1.9mg

Crispy Air Fryer Bacon

Prep Time: 3 minutes

Cook Time: 12 minutes

Total Time: 15 minutes

Servings: 6

Ingredients:

- 12 oz pack of bacon

Directions:

1. Lay bacon in an air fryer basket, bacon can overlap. Cook on 360 degrees Fahrenheit for 12-15 minutes, turning every 5 minutes. Remove and enjoy.

Notes:

- Keep an eye on that bacon. Some air fryers will cook bacon faster than others. Watch it closely to avoid overcooking.
- If you're cooking less than a pack of bacon, your bacon will cook much quicker, in about 8-10 minutes.
- Some air fryers are known for smoking while cooking bacon. Place a little water in the bottom of the basket or a piece of bread to soak up the grease can reduce the smoking. Also, always use a clean air fryer when cooking bacon or other greasy meats to reduce the amount of smoke.
- This method works for pork and turkey bacon.

- If you don’t want your bacon to curl, cook less at a time and lay them in a single layer. They’ll still curl a little.

Nutrition Facts:

Calories: 236kcal | Carbohydrates: 1g | Protein: 7g | Fat: 23g | Saturated Fat: 8g | Cholesterol: 37mg | Sodium: 375mg | Potassium: 112mg | Vitamin A: 21IU | Calcium: 3mg | Iron: 1mg

Easy Homemade Bagel

Prep Time: 5 minutes

Cook Time: 10 minutes

Total Time: 15 minutes

Servings: 4

Ingredients:

- 1 cup self-rising flour or 1 cup all-purpose flour, 1 and ½ baking powder, and ¼ tsp salt mixed together
- 1 cup Greek Yogurt
- 1 egg lightly beaten
- Toppings of your choice

Directions:

2. Combine self-rising flour and Greek Yogurt in a bowl and stir until they are fully

combined together. Once this is done you will want to place the dough on a floured surface and knead until you form a ball with the dough.

3. Separate the dough into 4 equal-sized pieces and then roll them into circles. Lightly flatten them and stick a hole in the middle.
4. Use a pastry brush and spread the egg over the bagel dough. Top with your favorite toppings. Bake in the Air fryer or oven.
5. Lightly spray the Air Fryer Basket with oil and place the bagels inside. Cook on 400 degrees Fahrenheit for 8-10 minutes or until tops are golden and the bagel is cooked through. Remove and allow it to cool.

Nutrition Facts:

Calories: 158kcal | Carbohydrates: 25g | Protein: 10g | Fat: 2g | Saturated Fat: 1g | Cholesterol: 43mg | Sodium: 34mg | Potassium: 117mg | Fiber: 1g | Sugar: 2g | Vitamin A: 59IU | Calcium: 66mg | Iron: 1mg

Flaky Air Fryer Donuts

Prep Time: 10 minutes

Cook Time: 10 minutes

Freezing Time: 15

Total Time: 35 minutes

Servings: 9

Ingredients:

- 2 puff pastry sheets defrosted
- 1 egg lightly beaten
- 4 Tbsp melted butter
- ½ cup white sugar
- ½ tsp cinnamon

Directions:

1. Roll out puff pastry on a lightly floured countertop and brush egg on one side of each pastry.
2. Lay the pieces of puff pastry on top of each other, making sure the sides brushed with egg are touching each other. Place in the freezer for 15 minutes.
3. After 15 minutes, remove pastry from the freezer and use a donut cutter or two cookie cutters to cut out donut shapes.
4. Place in air fryer basket and cook on 330 degrees Fahrenheit for 10 minutes, until the pastry has risen and is browned a bit.
5. While the pastry is cooking, combine white sugar and cinnamon in a bowl and set aside.

6. Once the pastry is finished cooking, brush with melted butter and dip in cinnamon and sugar mixture.
7. Serve and enjoy.

Notes:

1. Be sure to freeze the pastry together for at least 15 minutes.
2. A large air fryer will be able to hold about 6 donuts at a time. Place remaining cut donuts in the refrigerator or freezer so they remain cold while the donuts are air frying.
3. Preheat the air fryer for the most flakey donuts.
4. The donuts should be placed in a single layer in the basket and not touching.

Nutrition Facts:

Calories: 396kcal | Carbohydrates: 36g | Protein: 5g | Fat: 26g | Saturated Fat: 9g | Cholesterol: 32mg | Sodium: 188mg | Potassium: 40mg | Fiber: 1g | Sugar: 12g | Vitamin A: 184IU | Calcium: 11mg | Iron: 1mg

Air Fryer Cinnamon Rolls

Prep Time: 20 minutes

Cook Time: 9 minutes

Total Time: 29 minutes

Servings: 8

Ingredients:

- 1 pound frozen bread dough, thawed
- ¼ cup butter, melted and cooled
- ¾ cup brown sugar
- 1½ tablespoons ground cinnamon,
- Cream Cheese Glaze:
- 4 ounces cream cheese, softened
- 2 tablespoons butter, softened
- 1¼ cups powdered sugar

- ½ teaspoon vanilla

Directions:

1. Let the bread dough come to room temperature on the counter. On a lightly floured surface roll the dough into a 13-inch by 11-inch rectangle. Position the rectangle so the 13-inch side is facing you. Brush the melted butter all over the dough, leaving a 1-inch border uncovered along the edge farthest away from you.
2. Combine the brown sugar and cinnamon in a small bowl. Sprinkle the mixture evenly over the buttered dough, keeping the 1-inch border uncovered. Roll the dough into a log starting with the edge closest to you. Roll the dough tightly, making sure to roll evenly and push out any air pockets. When you get to the uncovered edge of the

dough, press the dough onto the roll to seal it together.

3. Cut the log into 8 pieces, slicing slowly with a sawing motion so you don't flatten the dough. Turn the slices on their sides and cover with a clean kitchen towel. Let the rolls sit in the warmest part of your kitchen for 1½ to 2 hours to rise.
4. To make the glaze, place the cream cheese and butter in a microwave-safe bowl. Soften the mixture in the microwave for 30 seconds at a time until it is easy to stir. Gradually add the powdered sugar and stir to combine. Add the vanilla extract and whisk until smooth. Set aside.
5. When the rolls have risen, pre-heat the air fryer to 350ºF.

6. Transfer 4 of the rolls to the air fryer basket. Air-fry for 5 minutes. Turn the rolls over and air-fry for another 4 minutes. Repeat with the remaining 4 rolls.
7. Let the rolls cool for a couple of minutes before glazing. Spread large dollops of cream cheese glaze on top of the warm cinnamon rolls, allowing some of the glaze to drip down the side of the rolls. Serve warm and enjoy!

Air Fryer Banana Bread Pizza

Prep Time: 10 minutes

Cook Time: 15 minutes

Total Time: 25 minutes

Servings: 16

Ingredients:

- 3 ripe bananas mashed
- 1 1/2 tsp baking powder
- 1/4 tsp baking soda
- 1 tbsp cinnamon
- 1 egg
- 1 cup brown sugar
- 3 1/2 cups flour
- 1 cup powdered sugar for rolling

Cream Cheese Layer:

- 1 8 oz cream cheese softened
- 2/3 cup sugar

Toppings:

- 1 21 oz can apple pie filling
- 1/2 cup pecans
- caramel syrup for drizzling

1. Directions:
2. In a mixing bowl, add ripe bananas, baking soda, baking powder, eggs, cinnamon, and brown sugar. Mix together.
3. Add flour to the mixture. Combine until a stiff dough is formed.

4. Divide dough in half. Make each half of the dough into a ball, rolling in powder sugar to prevent sticking to counter.
5. Flatten each ball into a round disc that can fit into the air fryer basket.
6. Spray 2 square piece of parchment paper with cooking spray and place one flat disc of dough on each. Make sure parchment paper is at least 2 inches bigger than the dough disc.

Cream Cheese Topping:

1. In a small bowl, place softened cream cheese and sugar. Stir together until there are no lumps.
2. Spread cream cheese mixture onto banana bread dough discs.

3. Top each pizza with half of the apple pie filling. Add pecans if desired

Air Fryer Instructions:

1. Preheat Air Fryer for at least 3 minutes at 350 degrees.
2. For the first pizza, carefully place parchment paper into air fryer basket. Cook banana bread pizza for 15 minutes. Lift pizza out by grabbing the ends of the parchment paper.
3. Allow to cool. Cook second pizza for 15 minutes.

Serving Suggestions:

1. Place Banana Bread Pizza on large plates and drizzle with caramel syrup.

Chick-Fil-A Crispy Chicken Sandwich Copycat

Prep Time: 30 minutes

Cook Time: 10minutes

Total Time: 40 minutes

Servings: 4

Ingredients:

- 4 chicken breast halves
- 1/2 cup pickle juice
- 1/4 cup water
- 1/2 cup milk
- 1 large egg
- oil for frying
- 4 hamburger buns

- Pickle, lettuce, tomato and cheese slices , for topping

For the breading:

- 1 cup all-purpose flour
- 3 Tablespoons powdered sugar
- 1/2 teaspoon paprika
- 1 teaspoon freshly ground black pepper
- 1/2 teaspoon chili powder
- 1/2 teaspoon salt
- 1/2 teaspoon baking powder
- 1-2 teaspoons cayenne pepper *optional, for a spicy chicken sandwich
- For the Chick-fil-A-sauce
- 1/2 cup mayonnaise

- 1 teaspoon dijon mustard
- 3 teaspoons yellow mustard
- 2 teaspoon barbecue sauce (hickory tastes the best)
- 2 Tablespoons honey
- 1/2 teaspoon garlic powder
- 1/2 teaspoon paprika
- 1 teaspoon lemon juice

Directions:

2. Marinate the chicken: combine the pickle juice and water in a ziplock bag. Add the chicken breast halves and marinate for 30 minutes.

3. Make the sauce: Make the Chick-fil-A sauce by combining all ingredients in a bowl. Mix well and set aside.
4. Next, in a large bowl mix the breading ingredients together: flour, powdered sugar, paprika, black pepper, chili powder, salt, and baking powder.
5. In another bowl mix the milk, and egg.
6. Add 2-3 cups of oil to a large saucepan and heat oil to about 350 degrees F.
7. Coat the chicken: Dip the marinated chicken into the egg mixture, and then coat in the flour breading mixture. Now "double-dip" by repeating this step and dipping that same chicken tender back into the egg mixture and then back into the flour again!

8. Pan fry: Place chicken in hot oil and fry for 3-4 minutes on each side. Remove to paper towel to dry.
9. Assemble Sandwich: Toast the sandwich buns. Grab the Chick-fil-A sauce and smooth it on both sides of the buns. Top with lettuce, cheese, and crispy chicken! Enjoy!

Nutrition Facts:

Calories: 579kcal | Carbohydrates: 62g | Protein: 21g | Fat: 27g | Saturated Fat: 4g | Cholesterol: 88mg | Sodium: 1286mg | Potassium: 391mg | Fiber: 2g | Sugar: 15g | Vitamin A: 525IU | Vitamin C: 1.7mg | Calcium: 147mg | Iron: 3.7mg

Popcorn Chicken

Prep Time: 15 minutes

Cook Time: 20 minutes

Total Time: 35minutes

Servings: 4

Ingredients:

- 2 boneless skinless chicken breasts cubed
- 2 tbsp flour
- 1 tsp garlic salt
- 1 cup buttermilk
- 1 cup panko crumbs
- pepper
- vegetable oil

Directions:

1. Add 1-2 inches of vegetable oil to a medium pan and heat on the medium setting.
2. Mix together flour and garlic salt in a small bowl. In another small bowl add buttermilk. In a third small bowl add the panko crumbs. Place the three bowls in a line.
3. Dip the chicken pieces in the flour mixture first followed by the buttermilk and lastly the panko crumbs. Dip all the chicken pieces making sure that all sides are coated with each ingredient. NOTE: for a double coating dip the pieces in the buttermilk a second time and again in the panko crumbs. If you're make a double coating you will need extra milk and panko crumbs.

4. Place a paper towel on a plate next to the stove near the hot oil.
5. Working in batches, place the chicken pieces in the hot oil. Fry for 3-4 minutes on each side or until golden brown. Once the pieces are done use tongs to remove them from the oil and place them on the paper towel lined plate
6. Serve warm with your favorite dipping sauce.

Nutrition Facts:

Calories 238.92 | Fat 5.75g | Saturated Fat 1.96g | Cholesterol 78.92mg | Sodium 885.32mg | Potassium 528.5mg | Carbohydrates 16.59g | Fiber 0.78g | Sugar 3.87g | Protein 28.3g

Chicken Cordon Bleu

Prep Time: 10 minutes

Cook Time: 30 minutes

Total Time: 40 minutes

Servings: 6

Ingredients

Chicken:

- 3 chicken breasts filled to form 6 thin pieces of chicken
- 6 slices ham turkey ham also works great
- 6 slices swiss cheese
- 1/2 cup bread crumbs
- 1/2 cup panko bread crumbs
- toothpicks

- cooking spray

Sauce:

- 2 tbsp butter
- 2 tbsp flour
- 3/4 cup milk
- 3/4 cup chicken broth
- 1/2 tsp salt
- pepper to taste
- 1 tsp dijon mustard
- 2 tbsp grated parmesan cheese

Directions:

1. Preheat the oven to 350. Spray a 9 x 9 baking dish with cooking spray. Mix the bread crumbs together on a plate or flat dish. To make each chicken roll up, layer

one slice of ham and one slice of swiss cheese on each of the chicken pieces. Roll up tightly, then roll in the bread crumb mixture. Secure with toothpicks and place in the prepared baking dish. Spray with cooking spray. Bake 30 - 35 minutes, or until cooked through.

2. When the chicken has about 15 minutes left, make the sauce. Melt the butter in a saucepan over medium heat. Add the flour and whisk to form a smooth paste. Cook 2-3 minutes, until golden. Add the milk, whisking constantly, until combined. Cook until slightly thickened, then slowly add the chicken broth while continuing to whisk constantly to prevent lumps. Whisk in the salt and pepper. When the sauce has thickened, remove from heat and whisk in

the dijon mustard and parmesan cheese until melted and combined. Serve chicken over pasta or rice and drizzle with sauce.

Nutrition Facts:

Calories 429 | Fat 21g | Saturated Fat 10g | Cholesterol 130mg | Sodium 1002mg | Potassium 610mg | Carbohydrates 15g | Sugar 2g | Protein 41g

Air Fryer Coconut Shrimp

Prep Time: 20 minutes

Cook Time: 20 minutes

Total Time: 40 minutes

Servings: 4 - 5

Ingredients:

Coconut Shrimp:

- 1 ¼ pound jumbo raw shrimp (peeled + deveined)
- 1 cup EACH: shredded sweetened coconut AND Panko crumbs
- 1/3 cup all-purpose flour
- 2 large eggs
- ½ teaspoon EACH: garlic powder AND salt

Sweet and tangy sauce:

- 1/3 cup sweet chili sauce
- 2 teaspoons mayo
- 1/2 lime, squeezed (more or less to taste)

Directions:

1. PREP: Rinse the shrimp under cold running water, then, pat them dry on paper towels. Set up a dredging station. The first bowl should contain the flour, garlic powder, and ½ teaspoon of salt (whisk to combine.) In the second bowl, add the two eggs and whisk to combine. The third bowl will contain the shredded coconut and the Panko breadcrumbs, toss or stir to combine.
2. DREDGE: Grab the shrimp by the tail, dredge it in the flour, shake off any excess.

Then, dip it in the egg mixture, and finally in the coconut mixture. Use your hands to press down so the crumbs adhere to the shrimp. Place the coated shrimp on a clean baking sheet. Continue with the remaining shrimp. At this point, you can freeze the shrimp for 30 minutes to make it easier to fry them or refrigerate until ready to fry. You can also fry or air fry them immediately.

3. AIR FRYER: Preheat the air fryer according to manufacturers' directions at 375ºF. Place the shrimp on a clean surface and spray the shrimp with coconut cooking spray (or any kind you like) place the sprayed side down in the air fryer and spray the other side with cooking spray. Cook the shrimp at 375ºF for 6-8 minutes or until they cook all

the way through, be sure to flip the shrimp around the halfway mark.

4. SAUCE: Combine the ingredients for the sauce in a bowl and whisk. You want to make sure to work the lumps out of the sauce completely. Taste and adjust with additional lime juice as desired. Serve with the shrimp!

Seared Steak with Truffle Herb Fries

Prep Time: 15 minutes

Cook Time: 35 minutes

Resting Time: 10 minutes

Total Time: 1 hour

Servings: 2

Ingredients

Seared Steak:

- 2 strip steaks
- kosher salt
- freshly cracked black pepper
- 3 to 4 tablespoons unsalted butter
- Truffle Herb Fries in the Air Fryer:
- 2 to 3 russet potatoes, thinly sliced

- olive oil for spritzing/brushing
- 1 teaspoon truffle salt
- 2 tablespoons chopped fresh parsley
- 2 tablespoons freshly grated parmesan cheese

Honey Dijon Aioli:

- ⅓ cup mayonnaise
- 1 garlic clove, minced
- 1 tablespoon dijon mustard
- 2 teaspoons honey

Directions:

Seared Steak:

1 Make sure your steaks sit out at room temperature for about 30 minutes.

2 Heat a cast iron skillet over medium-high heat - you want it hot! Season the steaks on both sides with the salt and pepper.

3 Add 2 tablespoons of butter to the hot skillet. It will sizzle and smoke and once it's all melted, add in the steaks. Cook for 3 minute, until deeply golden, then flip and cook for 3 minutes more. Add in the remaining butter. Once it melts, spoon it over top of the steaks for another 1 to 2 minutes. (almost medium doneness or medium well). Remove the steaks and let them rest for 10 to 15 minutes before slicing.

Truffle Herb Fries in the Air Fryer:

1 Place the sliced potatoes in a large bowl and cover with cold water. Let the potatoes sit in the water for 30 to 60 minutes.

Remove the potatoes and place them on kitchen towels - you want them completely dry! Pat them as dry as you can!

2 Preheat your air fryer to 375 degrees F. Place the potatoes on a baking sheet and spray or brush with olive oil. Place the fries in a single layer in your air fryer (you might have to do 2 batches!). Cook for 12 minutes, then gently flip the fries and cook for 5 to 6 minutes more.

3 Stir together the parsley and parmesan cheese. When the fries are done, place them on a plate or a sheet of parchment paper and sprinkle all over with the truffle salt immediately. Sprinkle with the herbs and parmesan mixture. Serve with the aioli.

4 If you do 2 batches, or if the fries are done before the steak, you can stick these in a 200 degree F oven until ready to eat!

Honey Dijon Aioli:

1 Whisk ingredients together until combined.

Air Fryer Zucchini Corn Fritters

Prep Time: 10 minutes

Cook Time: 12 minutes

Total Time: 22 minutes

Servings: 4

Ingredients:

- 2 medium zucchini
- 1 cup corn kernels
- 1 medium potato cooked
- 2 tbsp chickpea flour
- 2-3 garlic finely minced
- 1-2 tsp olive oil
- salt and pepper

For Serving:

- Ketchup or Yogurt tahini sauce

Directions:

1. Grate zucchini using a grater or food processor. In a mixing bowl, mix grated zucchini with a little salt and leave it for 10-15 min. Then squeeze out excess water from the zucchini using clean hands or using a cheesecloth.
2. Also, grate or mash the cooked potato*.
3. Combine zucchini, potato, corn, chickpea flour, garlic, salt, and pepper in a mixing bowl.
4. Roughly take 2 tbsp batter, give it a shape of a patty and place them on parchment paper**.

5. Lightly brush oil on the surface of each fritter. Preheat Air Fryer to 360F.
6. Place the fritters on the preheated Air Fryer mesh without touching each other. Cook them for 8 min.
7. Then turn the fritters and cook for another 3-4 min or until well done or till you get the desired color.
8. Serve warm with ketchup or yogurt tahini sauce

Notes:

- Cooking potato - cook the potato in a microwave oven for 3 min. Then place in cold water for a few minutes. Peel and then grate or mash.
- **Place the prepared patties on the parchment paper before cooking. It will

really help to brush the oil and then take them out without breaking or sticking to the bottom. (Please do not put the parchment paper inside the Fryer. The parchment paper is simply to keep the raw fritters before loading them into the Air Fryer)

- Add more flour if necessary. You can also use all purpose flour instead of chickpea flour.
- Yogurt tahini sauce - mix 1/2 cup yogurt with 1 tsp tahini and season with salt according to taste.

Air Fryer Egg Fried Rice

Prep Time: 5 minutes

Cook Time: 15 minutes

Total Time: 20 minutes

Servings: 4

Ingredients:

- 3 c rice cooked and cold
- 1 c frozen vegetables , carrot, corn, broccoli and edamame
- ⅓ c coconut aminos
- 1 T oil
- 2 eggs scrambled (optional)

Directions:

1. To make your air fryer fried rice, put your cold rice into an large bowl.

2. Then add your frozen vegetables to the rice bowl.
3. If you are using egg or another protein, add it to the rice bowl now.
4. Next up, you are going to add the coconut aminos and oil to your bowl.
5. Mix, mix, mix until well combined. Then transfer to the rice mixture to an oven safe container.
6. Place that container into your air fryer. Cook the air fryer fried rice at 360 degrees F for 15 minutes. You can stir 3 times through the 15 minutes.
7. Enjoy!

Nutrition Facts:

Calories: 618kcal | Carbohydrates: 121g | Protein: 14g | Fat: 7g | Saturated Fat: 1g | Cholesterol: 82mg | Sodium: 512mg | Potassium: 286mg | Fiber: 4g | Sugar: 1g | Vitamin A: 2429IU | Vitamin C: 5mg | Calcium: 63mg | Iron: 2mg

Air Fryer Toasted Pierogies

Prep Time: 15 minutes

Cook Time: 12 minutes

Total Time: 27 minutes

Servings: 6

Ingredients:

- 1 bag store bought frozen Perogies
- 2 cups Italian-style bread crumbs
- 1 egg
- cup buttermilk
- Olive Oil Spray
- Parmesan cheese optional

Directions:

1 Whisk together egg and buttermilk. Dip Perogi in the egg/milk mixture and then cover with breadcrumbs. Repeat with all perogies.

2 Add perogies to the air fryer basket and spray with olive oil spray. Close the fryer basket and press power. Set the temperature to 400 degrees F and time to 12 minutes. Halfway through, pause and turn the perogies over. Add additional spray, if needed.

3 Garnish with additional Parmesan cheese and serve hot.

Air Fryer Chicken Parmesan

Prep Time: 10 minutes

Cook Time: 20 minutes

Total Time: 30 minutes

Servings: 4

Ingredients:

- 1 Lb Chicken Breast (about 4 small breasts)
- 1/4 Cup White whole wheat flour (or GF all purpose)
- 1/3 Cup Italian seasoned bread crumbs (GF if needed)
- 1/3 cup Italian seasoned Panko (GF if needed)
- 1/2 tsp Italian seasoning
- 3/4 tsp Salt

- 1/2 Cup + 2 Tbsp Parmesan Cheese, grated and divided
- 2 Large eggs
- 1/3 Cup Marinara sauce
- 1/2 Cup Mozzarella cheese, Grated
- Sliced basil, for garnish

Directions:

1. Place the chicken between two layers of parchment paper and use a rolling pin or meat mallet to flatten about 1/2 inch thick.
2. Place the flour in a large, rimmed plate. Then, mix the bread crumbs, panko, Italian seasoning, salt, and 1/3 cup of the Parmesan cheese together and pour into another rimmed plate. Finally, whisk the eggs in a medium bowl.

3 Use one hand to dredge the chicken in the flour and then the egg, shaking off the excess. Use our other hand to cover the chicken in the panko mixture, pressing it on to coat it well. Place into the mesh air-fryer basket and repeat with all remaining chicken.

4 Bake at 400 degrees until the chicken starts to brown and get crispy, about 8-10 minutes.

5 Then, spread the marinara sauce on top of the chicken, followed by the rest of the Parmesan cheese and the mozzarella cheese. Bake for another 2-4 minutes, until the cheese is melted and the chicken reads 165 degrees F on the inside.

6 Sprinkle on basil and DEVOUR!

Nutrition Facts:

Calories: 375kcal | Carbohydrates: 18.9g | Protein: 38.6g | Fat: 16.1g | Saturated Fat: 6.4g | Cholesterol: 193.4mg | Sodium: 1396mg | Potassium: 26.8mg | Fiber: 1.6g | Sugar: 2g

Crispy Air Fryer Tofu

Prep Time: 30 minutes

Cook Time: 10 minutes

Total Time: 40 minutes

Servings: 4

Ingredients:

- 1 lb block of extra firm tofu, pressed for 30 minutes then cut into 1″ cubes (16 oz.)
- 1 teaspoon garlic powder
- ½ teaspoon onion powder
- 1 teaspoon paprika
- ½ teaspoon sea salt
- 2 teaspoons cornstarch
- ½ tablespoon light soy sauce or liquid aminos

- ½ teaspoon sesame oil or any oil
- ¼ teaspoon ground black pepper

Directions:

1 In a medium size bowl place the pressed and cubed tofu. Add in liquid aminos and toss to coat. Add in all of the other seasoning ingredients and toss to thoroughly combine.

2 Place in your air fryer in a single row, so that all the tofu has a little bit of space around each piece. Set your air fryer to 400°F. Cook for 10 minutes, shaking the basket after 5 minutes, then continuing to cook.

3 Remove after tofu is cooked. Allow to cool for a few minutes then serve. Enjoy!

Nutrition Facts:

Calories: 110kcal | Carbohydrates: 5g | Protein: 11g | Fat: 6g | Saturated Fat: 1g | Sodium: 416mg | Potassium: 20mg | Fiber: 1g | Sugar: 1g | Vitamin A: 246IU | Calcium: 142mg | Iron: 1mg

Air Fryer Southwestern Egg Rolls

Prep Time: 20 minutes

Cook Time: 12 minutes

Total Time: 32 minutes

Servings: 8

Ingredients:

- 1/4 red onion chopped
- 2-3 garlic cloves chopped
- 16 egg roll wrappers
- 1/2 red pepper chopped
- 1/2 yellow pepper chopped
- 1/2 orange pepper chopped
- 1/4 cup shredded cheese
- oz low-sodium black beans (drained)

- 1 can diced tomatoes and chilis (drained)
- 1 cup frozen kernel corn
- 2 teaspoons cilantro chopped
- 1/2 lime juice
- 1/4 packet Taco Seasoning
- cooking oil
- cup of water

Avocado Ranch Dip:

- oz sour cream
- 1 avocado
- 1/2 packet Hidden Valley Ranch Dip Seasoning

Directions:

1 Heat a skillet on medium-high heat. Add the garlic and onions. Cook for 2-3 minutes until fragrant.

2 Add all of the peppers to the skillet. Mix well. Cook for 1-2 minutes

3 Add the black beans, corn, tomatoes, and cheese. Cook for 2-3 minutes.

4 Drizzle the fresh lime juice throughout. Add the cilantro and taco seasoning. Stir.

5 Lay the egg roll wrappers on a flat surface. Dip a cooking brush in water. Glaze each of the egg roll wrappers with the wet brush along the edges. This will soften the crust and make it easier to roll.

6 Use 2 egg rolls for each. You can choose to double roll the egg rolls to prevent them

from leaking. If the brand of egg roll wrappers you purchased is pretty thick, you may only need one wrapper and no need to double up.

7 Load the mixture into each of the wrappers.

8 Fold the wrappers diagonally to close. Press firmly on the area with the filling, cup it to secure it in place. Fold in the left and right sides as triangles. Fold the final layer over the top to close. Use the cooking brush to wet the area and secure it in place. Spray each egg roll with cooking oil.

9 Load the egg rolls into the pan of the Air Fryer. Spray with cooking oil.

10 Cook for 8 minutes at 380 degrees. Flip the egg rolls. Cook for an additional 4 minutes. Cool before serving.

Nutrition Facts:

Calories: 265kcal | Carbohydrates: 39g | Protein: 11g | Fat: 3g

Air Fryer Buffalo Cauliflower from Raw or Frozen

Prep Time: 5 minutes

Cook Time: 20 minutes

Total Time: 25 minutes

Servings: 2

Ingredients:

- 2 cups cauliflower frozen florets, thawed, or raw
- olive oil spray or butter
- ½ cup hot sauce
- ¾ cup nutritional yeast or panko breadcrumbs (optional)

Directions:

1 Set your air fryer to 400° F.

2. Pour 2 cups of cauliflower into a large bowl. Spray liberally with cooking spray, shaking to make sure it is well coated on all sides, then add your hot sauce. Toss and stir until all of your cauliflower is coated with hot sauce, then add your nutritional yeast and toss one last time.
3. Add your cauliflower to the basket of your air fryer, and set the cook timer for 20 minutes.
4. Toss your cauliflower every 5 minutes to promote even cooking and browning. Your cauliflower should be nicely browned and crispy when it's done. If cauliflower seems soggy, continue cooking for 5 minute increments.

Nutrition Facts:

Calories: 87kcal | Carbohydrates: 12g | Protein: 10g | Fat: 1g | Saturated Fat: 1g | Sodium: 1870mg | Potassium: 629mg | Fiber: 6g | Sugar: 2g | Vitamin C: 48mg | Calcium: 22mg | Iron: 1mg

Air Fryer Chicken Breast Cutlets

Prep Time: 10 minutes

Cook Time: 10 minutes

Total Time: 20 minutes

Servings: 6

Ingredients:

- 1.5 pounds chicken breast butterflied
- 2 cups panko bread crumbs or make your own
- 1 egg
- 1/2 cup Kodiak Cakes Flapjack Mix
- 1/2 tsp salt divided
- 1/2 tsp onion powder divided
- 1/2 tsp pepper divided

- 3/4 tsp paprika divided
- 1/4 cup parmesan cheese

Directions:

1 To begin cooking the air fryer chicken breast, preheat Air Fryer to 390F. Spray roasting pan with olive oil spray.

2 Trim chicken breast of excess fat. Be sure to butterfly chicken breasts or pound to no thicker than 1/4 inch. This is an important step to make sure the chicken cooks thoroughly.

3 Measure out breadcrumbs and Kodiak cake mix into two separate bowls. Season breadcrumbs and Kodiak cake mix evenly with spices. Add parmesan cheese to the breadcrumb bowl. Put egg in third bowl and scramble with a fork. Line up the

bowls in order of Kodiak Cakes mix, egg, breadcrumbs.

4 Dredge chicken in pancake mix then dip and coat into eggs. Coat with breadcrumb mix on all sides.

5 Place chicken in air fryer basket and cook at 390F for 4 minutes. Flip and cook for 2-4 minutes depending on thickness of chicken. Chicken is cooked at 165F and is best determined with a meat thermometer. Cook until done.

Notes:

- Temperatures for air fryers do vary. Use this recipe temperature and time as a suggestion and adjust to your own model.
- To ensure proper and even cooking, cook food in one layer to make sure both sides

get crispy. Make sure you give each piece a bit of space to optimize crispiness.

- Spray your tray and food with coconut oil spray. It is better for your air fryer than using traditional cooking spray.
- Flip your chicken halfway (four minutes per side) for optimum crisp.
- Breading won't stick? Make sure you dry your chicken thoroughly before seasoning and breading.

Nutrition Facts:

Calories: 363kcal | Carbohydrates: 35.3g | Protein: 35.9g | Fat: 7.9g

Quinoa Burgers

Prep Time: 30 minutes

Cook Time: 10 minutes

Total Time: 40 minutes

Servings: 4

Ingredients:

- 1 CUP quinoa red, white or multi-colored
- 1½ CUPS water
- 1 TEASPOON salt
- freshly ground black pepper
- 1½ CUPS rolled oats OR whole-wheat breadcrumbs
- eggs lightly beaten
- ¼ CUP minced white onion

- ½ CUP crumbled feta cheese
- ¼ CUP chopped fresh chives
- salt and freshly ground black pepper
- vegetable or canola oil
- whole-wheat hamburger buns
- arugula
- SLICES tomato sliced

Cucumber Yogurt Dill Sauce:

- 1 CUP cucumber finely diced
- 1 CUP Greek yogurt
- 2 TSP lemon juice
- ¼ TSP salt
- freshly ground black pepper
- 1 TBSP fresh dill chopped

- 1 TBSP olive oil

Directions:

1 Make the quinoa: Rinse the quinoa in cold water in a saucepan, swirling it with your hand until any dry husks rise to the surface. Drain the quinoa as well as you can and then put the saucepan on the stovetop. Turn the heat to medium-high and dry the quinoa on the stovetop, shaking the pan regularly until you see the quinoa moving easily and can hear the seeds moving in the pan. Add the water, salt and pepper. Bring the liquid to a boil and then reduce the heat to low or medium-low. You should just see a few bubbles, not a boil. Cover with a lid, leaving it askew (or if you have pour spouts, just put the lid on the pot) and simmer for 20

minutes. Turn the heat off and fluff the quinoa with a fork. If there's any liquid left in the bottom of the pot, place it back on the burner for another 3 minutes or so. Spread the cooked quinoa out on a sheet pan to cool.

2 Combine the room temperature quinoa in a large bowl with the oats, eggs, onion, cheese and herbs. Season with salt and pepper and mix well. Shape the mixture into 4 patties. Add a little water or a few more rolled oats to get the mixture to be the right consistency to make patties.

3 Spray both sides of the patties generously with oil and transfer them to the air fryer basket in one layer (you will probably have to cook these burgers in batches depending on the size of your air fryer). Air-fry each

batch at 400ºF for 10 minutes, flipping the burgers over halfway through the cooking time.

4 While the burgers are cooking, make the cucumber yogurt dill sauce by mixing all the ingredients in a bowl.

5 Build your burger on the whole-wheat hamburger buns with arugula, tomato and the cucumber yogurt dill sauce.

Air Fried Jamaican Jerk Pork

Prep Time: 10 minutes

Cook Time: 20 minutes

Marinate Time: 4 hours

Total Time: 4 hours 30 minutes

Servings: 4

Ingredients:

- 1.5 lbs pork butt chopped into large 3 inch pieces
- ¼ cup jerk paste
- oil for spraying basket

Directions:

1 Rub pork pieces with jerk paste and allow it to marinate pork for 4-24 hours in the refrigerator. The longer the better.

2. Preheat air fryer to 390 degrees F. Spray the bottom of the basket to ensure they dont stick.
3. Remove pork and allow to rest at room temp for 20 minutes. Place in air fryer ensuring they are spaced apart. Set time for 20 minutes, flip halfway.
4. Remove from air fryer and allow to sit for 5-10 minutes before cutting.
5. Enjoy.

Nutrition Facts:

Calories: 234kcal | Protein: 31g | Fat: 9g | Saturated Fat: 3g | Sodium: 160mg | Potassium: 576mg

Air Fryer Salsa Chicken Taquitos

Prep Time: 5 minutes

Cook Time: 20 minutes

Total Time: 25minutes

Servings: 6

Ingredients:

- shredded cooked chicken from 1 roasted or rotisserie chicken
- 1/2 cup salsa, or more to taste
- 20 soft flour tortillas (fajita size)
- 1-1/2 cups shredded cheese
- olive oil spray

Directions:

1 In a mixing bowl, add the shredded chicken (about 4 cups) and 1/2 to 2/3 cup of salsa

or more and toss until evenly coated. Add more salsa as needed.

2 Working in batches, place a few tortillas down onto a clean surface. On 1/3 of the tortilla, place some of the salsa chicken and a little cheese.

3 Starting on the end with the chicken and cheese, fold it over and roll tightly before placing each one onto a rimmed metal baking sheet. Repeat with the remaining tortillas, chicken and cheese until all 20 are rolled.

4 Then spray all of the rolled taquitos with olive oil spray.

5 Preheat you air-fryer to 350-360° and working in batches of 4 or 5 taquitos at a time (any extra room in the basket could

cause them to unroll) air-fry for 4 to 5 mintues or until crispy and golden brown.

6 Repeat with the remaining taquitos.

7 Serve as is or with desired toppings

Nutrition Facts:

Calories: 869 | Total Fat: 35g | Saturated Fat: 12g | Trans Fat: 0g | Unsaturated Fat: 20g | Cholesterol: 113mg | Sodium: 1183mg | Carbohydrates: 93g | Fiber: 6g | Sugar: 1g | Protein: 43g

Air Fryer Falafel

Prep Time: 15 minutes

Cook Time: 30 minutes

Refrigerate Time: 2 hours

Total Time: 2 hours 45 minutes

Servings: 4

Ingredients:

- 1 (15.5 ounce) can chickpeas, rinsed and drained
- 1 small yellow onion, quartered
- cloves garlic, roughly chopped
- 1/3 cup roughly chopped parsley
- 1/3 cup roughly chopped cilantro
- 1/3 cup chopped scallions

- 1 teaspoon cumin
- 1/2 teaspoon kosher salt
- 1/8 teaspoon crushed red pepper flakes
- 1 teaspoon baking powder
- tablespoons all purpose flour, plus more for dusting
- olive oil spray

Optional for serving:

- hummus, sliced tomatoes, sliced cucumber, thinly sliced red onion, pita, tahini, etc

Directions:

1 Dry the chickpeas on paper towels.

2 Place the onions and garlic in the bowl of a food processor fitted with a steel blade.

Add the parsley, scallions, cilantro, cumin, salt, and red pepper flakes.

3 Process until blended 30 to 60 seconds, then add the chickpeas and pulse 2 to 3 times until just blended, but not pureed.

4 Sprinkle in the baking powder and the flour, scape the sides of the bowl down with a spatula and pulse 2 to 3 times.

5 Transfer to a bowl and refrigerate, covered, 2 to 3 hours.

6 Form the falafel mixture into 12 balls, if it's too sticky add some flour to your hands and your work surface.

7 Preheat the air fryer 350F.

8 Spray the falafel with oil. Cook 14 minutes, in batches until golden brown, turning halfway.

Notes:

- Refrigerate for up to 4 days. Freeze uncooked balls for up to 6 months. Defrost in the refrigerator overnight before air frying.

Nutrition Facts:

Calories: 134kcal, Carbohydrates: 24g, Protein: 6g, Fat: 2g, Sodium: 403mg, Fiber: 4g, Sugar: 1g

Air Fryer Fish

Prep Time: 5 minutes

Cook Time: 15 minutes

Total Time: 20 minutes

Servings: 4

Ingredients:

- 1 lb. white fish fillets (not more than ½ inch thick)
- 1 large egg
- ½ cup yellow cornmeal
- 1 tsp paprika
- ½ tsp garlic powder
- ½ tsp black pepper
- 1 tsp coarse salt

- oil spray
- lemon and parsley for garnish (Optional)

Directions:

1 Preheat the air fryer for at least 3 minutes to 400 F. Whisk the egg in a shallow pan. In another shallow pan, combine the cornmeal and spices thoroughly.

2 Pat the fish completely dry. Dip the fish fillets into the egg – allow the excess to drip back into the pan. Then press the fish into the cornmeal mixture until well coated on both sides.

3 Place the coated fish into the preheated air fryer basket. Spritz lightly with oil. Cook for 10 minutes – stopping midway to flip the fish to ensure even cooking. If you notice dry spots, this is the time to spritz with a

bit more oil. Return the basket to the air fryer and cook 5-7 minutes or until the fish is cooked through.

4 Once done, squeeze lightly with lemon and sprinkle with parsley or top with hot sauce as desired. Serve immediately.

Nutrition Facts:

Calories: 191kcal | Carbohydrates: 15g | Protein: 24g | Fat: 3g | Saturated Fat: 1g | Cholesterol: 95mg | Sodium: 662mg | Potassium: 561mg | Fiber: 2g | Sugar: 1g | Vitamin A: 359IU | Vitamin C: 1mg | Calcium: 25mg | Iron: 1mg

Air Fryer Chicken Tenders

Prep Time: 15 minutes

Cook Time: 15 minutes

Total Time: 30 minutes

Servings: 4

Ingredients:

- 1 lb chicken tenders
- ½ cup breadcrumbs like Panko
- ½ tsp salt or to taste
- ½ tsp pepper or to taste
- ½ tsp garlic powder
- large eggs beaten
- ½ cup all-purpose flour

Directions:

1 Prepare the dredge: Preheat the air fryer to 400F. Grab 3 shallow plates. Mix the breadcrumbs, salt, pepper, and garlic powder in one of the plates. Beat the eggs in the second plate, and add the flour to the third plate.

2 Dredge the tenders: Coat each tender in flour, then the beaten egg, and finally the breadcrumb mixture.

3 Air fry the tenders: Add the tenders to the air fryer basket and lightly spray them with cooking spray. Cook for 8 minutes, flip the tenders, spray with cooking spray, and cook for another 7 minutes or until golden brown. You might have to do this in batches if you can't fit all the chicken in one go.

4. Serve: Serve with your favorite dipping sauce.

Nutrition Facts:

Calories: 302kcal | Carbohydrates: 22g | Protein: 33g | Fat: 8g | Saturated Fat: 2g | Cholesterol: 231mg | Sodium: 582mg | Potassium: 521mg | Fiber: 1g | Sugar: 1g

Air Fryer Baked Apples

Prep Time: 5 minutes

Cook Time: 15 minutes

Total Time: 20 minutes

Servings: 2

Ingredients:

- 2 Apples
- 1 tsp Butter, melted
- ½ tsp Cinnamon

Topping:

- ⅓ cup Old Fashioned / Rolled Oats
- 1 tbsp Butter, melted
- 1 tbsp Maple Syrup (or honey or rice malt syrup)

- 1 tsp Wholemeal / Whole Wheat Flour, (can sub for almond meal or all purpose flour / plain flour)
- ½ tsp Cinnamon

Directions:

1 Preheat the air fryer on 180C / 350F by either using the preheat setting or running your air fryer for 5 minutes on that temperature.

2 Cut apples in half through the stem and use a knife or a spoon to remove the core, stem and seeds. Brush a tsp of butter evenly over the cut sides of the apples, then sprinkle over ½ tsp of cinnamon.

3 Mix topping ingredients together in a small bowl, then spoon on top of the apple halves evenly.

4 Place the apple halves carefully into the air fryer basket, then cook for 15 minutes or until softened.

5 Serve warm with ice cream or cream if desired.

Nutrition Facts:

Calories 247; Fat 9g; Cholesterol 20mg; Sodium 65mg; Carbohydrates 43g; Fiber 7g; Sugar 25g; Protein 3g

Lightning Source UK Ltd.
Milton Keynes UK
UKHW021321011222
413202UK00012B/113

9 798456 764591